DISCOVERING VIKINGS

Richard Platt

Illustrations by Nick Harris

ReD KiTE

First published in the UK in 2008 by Red Kite Books,
an imprint of Haldane Mason Ltd
PO Box 34196, London NW10 3YB
www.haldanemason.com

ISBN: 978-1-905339-04-4 (with helmet)
ISBN: 978-1-905339-05-1 (without helmet)

A HALDANE MASON BOOK
Art Director: Ron Samuel
All original artwork by Nick Harris

1 3 5 7 9 8 6 4 2

Printed in China

Contents

Cold Water Pirates

In Europe's cold north-western corner lie the Scandinavian countries of Denmark, Sweden, Finland and Norway. A thousand years ago these lands were the homes of a hardy race of farmers and seafarers. Their daring raids and long sea voyages made them famous – and feared.

The people of western and southern Europe scarcely noticed their northern neighbours until about AD 800. The lands of Scandinavia were cold and damp, and not good enough to be worth invading. The Scandinavian people themselves were more curious: Swedish merchants moved east to trade with Russians. But when these northern people turned to piracy, the world at last paid attention to them and gave them a name. In fact, they called them many names, some of them very rude. Among the most polite were 'Norsemen' or 'Northmen'. But to most people they were 'Vikings'. The name comes from *vikingr*, which means 'pirate' in early Scandinavian languages.

In their sleek longships, the Viking pirates could cross the chilly northern seas quickly. Expert navigators, they relied on the wind, sun, stars and ocean currents to guide them. When they landed, they swooped on defenceless coastal villages. Killing or capturing those who resisted, they searched for anything valuable. They took gold and silver – and farm animals, too, for these were scarce. Then they returned to their ships, and disappeared as quickly as they had arrived. These lightning raids continued for some 250 years, from about AD 800 to 1050.

To the Christian people of Europe, the raids were especially frightening, for the Vikings were pagans (they did not worship Jesus Christ). Instead they prayed to many gods, including Thor. One of the days of the week is still named in his honour – guess which one. As Vikings mingled with Christian people (and enslaved some of them), they learned about the Bible (the Christians' holy book). Soon they were themselves spreading the Christian story.

Vikings once had a bloody reputation, and their raids were certainly brutal and deadly. Recently, though, historians have begun to forgive their violent past. Instead, they stress the Vikings' achievements in art, craft and exploration. Vikings were the first European people to visit America. Their influence stretched far in other directions, too: in the east to Turkey and in the south to the Mediterranean Sea.

A true picture of the Vikings lies somewhere in between these two views. Part pirate, part farmer, part artist, part explorer, Vikings and the impact they made on the world will never be forgotten.

This book is to be returned on or before
the last date stamped below.

LIBREX

Viking Homelands

Norway Deep inlets called fjords cut fine harbours in Norway's ragged, mountainous coast. A line of islands protected the fjords from North Sea storms. Harsh, cold winters made Norway a cruel place to live. Farming was difficult even on the few small areas of flat, fertile land.

Finland In the country we now call Finland there were a few Swedish Viking settlements. Mostly misty bogs, lakes and forests, only a narrow strip of Finland along the Baltic Sea's east coast was good enough for farming.

Denmark The most southern and warmest of the Viking lands, Denmark was once covered in dark forests. Clearing them made rich farmland. Few Danes lived more than 55 km (35 miles) from the sea, or 30 m (100 ft) above it. The powerful kings who ruled Denmark controlled much of southern Sweden, too.

Sweden Viking Sweden covered only the bottom right and left corners of the modern country. It was a land of lakes and forests, with a coast of inlets and islands on the Baltic Sea. One of the biggest islands, Gotland, had rich farms.

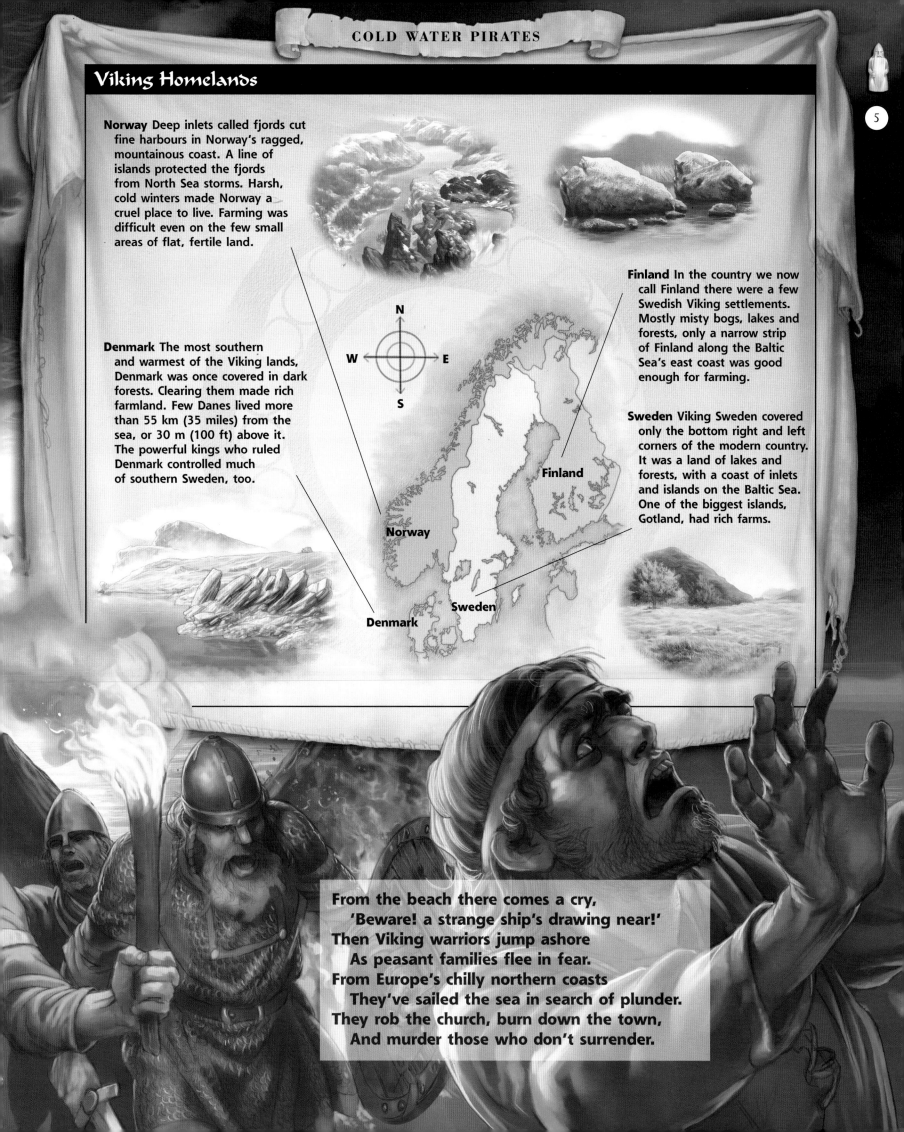

N
W E
S

Norway

Finland

Sweden

Denmark

From the beach there comes a cry,
'Beware! a strange ship's drawing near!'
Then Viking warriors jump ashore
As peasant families flee in fear.
From Europe's chilly northern coasts
They've sailed the sea in search of plunder.
They rob the church, burn down the town,
And murder those who don't surrender.

Viking Attack!

Viking raids began with a lightning attack on a tiny island off England's north-east coast. Called Lindisfarne, the island was the site of a wealthy monastery. On Saturday, 8 June 793, raiders – probably from Norway – stormed up the sandy beaches . . .

When the Vikings returned to their longships loaded with plunder, their swords dripped with the monks' blood. The deadly Lindisfarne raid was a great success for them. It was a greater shock to the English people. One wrote that:

'Never before has such terror appeared in Britain as we have now suffered from a pagan race, nor was it thought that such an attack could be made from the sea. Behold the church of St Cuthbert spattered with the blood of the priests . . . robbed of all its ornaments.'

▲ **Longboats:** Viking ships were light, so their crews could haul them up on the beaches, above the high tide, while they raided.

The raiders came back the following year and attacked another monastery nearby. This time they were not so lucky. Their leader was killed and storms wrecked at least one of their ships. Those who did not drown were killed when they swam ashore. This setback discouraged the raiders from attacking England again. Instead they looked further west, attacking the west coast of Scotland and then Ireland.

These first 'hit-and-run' raids took place in the summer, when the seas were calmest. But gradually, the raiders became more daring. They no longer returned to their homelands between each raid. Instead they stayed close to their targets in winter camps, called longphorts. In these strongholds the Vikings

6

were safe from attack. When spring came they could quickly start their raids again.

Viking raiders were also striking places farther to the south, and on mainland Europe. In 834 they swooped on the Dorestad in the Netherlands. It was northern Europe's biggest market town. Eleven years later they boldly sailed up the river Seine to Paris. There the French (called Frankish at the time) king, Charles the Bald, paid the raiders three tonnes of silver to spare the city from further raids.

The Vikings' French victims complained that:

'The number of ships grows: the endless stream of Vikings never ceases to increase. Everywhere the Christians are victims of massacres, burnings, plunderings: the Vikings conquer all in their path, and no one resists them: . . . countless ships sail up the Seine and the evil grows in the whole region. Paris is taken, and every town besieged.'

Danish Vikings sailed on around the French coast. They raided Normandy and Brittany before moving south to attack Spain. From there they cruised into

▸ **Treasure:** Vikings attacked places like the monastery at Lindisfarne because they knew they would find treasure. Though the monks were poor, monasteries could grow rich from gifts and by farming.

the Mediterranean to attack the towns of southern France and Italy.

Nor had they forgotten England. From 835, Viking raiders from Denmark again terrified people along England's east and south coasts. Within thirty years, the Viking raiders had become settlers and had made their homes there. Soon the Danes ruled most of eastern England. The English fought back, kicking out the last Viking King, Eirik Bloodaxe, in 954. Attacks began again soon after, when a Danish messenger brought these chilling words:

'You must send treasure quickly in return for peace. It will be better for you all to buy off an attack with treasure rather than face men as fierce as us in battle.'

Terrified, the English paid up. When the Vikings returned three years later, they paid again . . . and again. In the end, Viking power grew so great that Danish kings once more controlled England. Their rule ended only in 1066 when another invasion gave England a new king – this time from France!

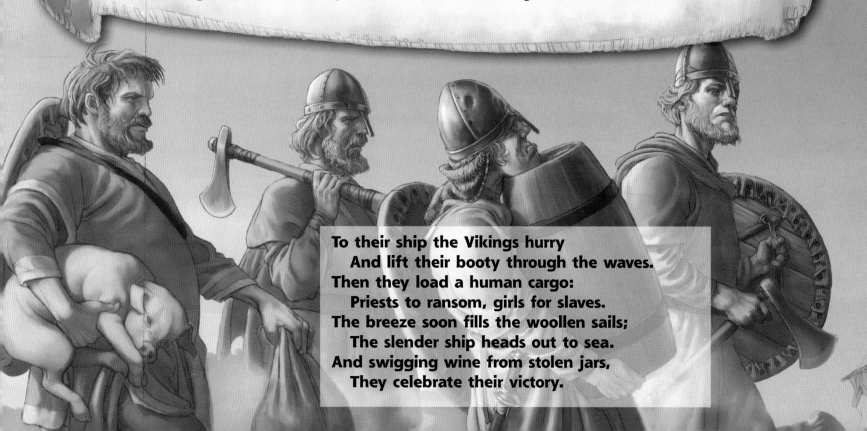

To their ship the Vikings hurry
 And lift their booty through the waves.
Then they load a human cargo:
 Priests to ransom, girls for slaves.
The breeze soon fills the woollen sails;
 The slender ship heads out to sea.
And swigging wine from stolen jars,
 They celebrate their victory.

Everyday Life

Harsh living conditions made the Viking people strong and independent. In their remote farm homes, families had to work together just to survive. Wealthier families had slaves to help them, and Viking chiefs and kings lived well, served and supplied by the people they ruled and protected.

Though we think of them as sea warriors, Viking people were more often farmers and fishermen. Most lived in scattered family groups, each a long way from their nearest neighbour. Life was not easy for a Viking family. Every year was a constant struggle against nature, for in these northern regions winters are long. Each summer everyone worked hard to produce enough food to last through the dark, cold months that followed.

There was no room for a 'charcoal-chewer' – someone who sat by the fire and did no work. There was a task for everyone except the sick,

◄ **Toys:** Children played with toys that were mostly carved from wood. Animals – usually horses – were popular. Wooden swords were accurate copies of real weapons.

the very old and the very young. With so much to do, it was fortunate that families were large. Besides their parents, children lived with their grandparents, uncles and aunts, and adopted brothers and sisters. If the family was well-off there would be servants and perhaps slaves too. Freemen who were not related to the family also lived on the farm. As well as wages, their work earned them housing and food.

Women played a very important part in the life of a Viking family. When a man left his home to travel for trade or raiding, his wife took charge, controlling everything. The sign of her importance was the key to the family treasure chest, which hung from her belt. Even when their husbands were at home, women held the keys to barns and food stores.

Women worked to prepare food for the large families. Their other traditional task was making textiles. They spun and wove to make clothing and other kinds of fabrics, such as sails for ships and sheets for beds (see page 22).

Children learned at a very young age the jobs they would do later in life. Almost as soon as they could stand, there were small tasks for them. For schooling they just watched their parents at work and copied what they did. By the age of 12 childhood was over, and they were adults.

▲ **Weightlifting:** many men's games were fitness or strength coompetitions. Rock lifting was a favourite: huge boulders said to be lifted by outlaw Grettir the Strong are still landmarks in Iceland.

Vikings valued independence and bravery – not just in adults, but in their children as well. They smiled at what we might now call 'bad behaviour' such as disobedience and violence, because it showed that a child had spirit and strength of character.

By contrast, Vikings expected their slaves to be completely obedient, and to do the hardest, nastiest tasks. Some even gave up their lives to serve their masters and mistresses. At funerals slaves were sometimes executed. Buried with their owners, they continued to serve them in the afterlife (see page 24). Not all Viking slaves suffered, for slavery did not always last forever. Some slaves received wages and could buy their freedom; or their masters might free them as a reward for a good deed.

In the winter, the pace of life changed in the Viking home. As cold weather set in there was much less work to do. Crafts such as weaving continued, but families had more time to spend in eating and drinking, storytelling and entertaining. Life was very different for the powerful chieftains who controlled the Scandinavian countries, and the kings who ruled them. These lucky people often owned much land and grew wealthy from the crops and animals it produced. Or they became rich from the goods and money they received as tribute – a kind of tax – from lesser folk.

On reaching home the Viking chief
Learns some very special news.
His wife has given him a son
While he was on his year-long cruise.
'I name him "Eadred",' shouts the chief.
'He'll be a warrior, just like me.
I'll make him soon a worthy sword:
Together they'll be legendary.'

Tools and Weapons

Viking blacksmiths were expert iron-workers. At roaring forges they hammered out axes and scythes, and swords of extraordinary beauty. These legendary weapons were the most treasured possessions of Viking warriors, who gave them nicknames that praised their strength and sharpness.

The forests and swamps of Scandinavia provided Viking smiths with everything they needed to make useful tools and sharp weapons. From the forests came the charcoal they used for fuel. The swamps provided the iron: smiths found it as rusty-red pea-sized lumps beneath the top layer of peat.

Collecting this 'bog iron' and smelting it (heating it in a makeshift furnace) produced spongy lumps of crude iron. Smiths made it purer and stronger by heating and hammering again and again. Smelting wasn't easy. To make enough metal for a single axe head required 160 kg (350 lb) of wood – twice the weight of the smith. The difficulty of making iron meant that the metal was very precious. Smiths sold to farmers curved scythes for reaping grain, axes to clear the forests, and ploughs that cut easily through heavy clay soil.

But it was weapons that made Viking smiths famous. To make strong swords, the smiths twisted together bundles of iron bars. They heated and hammered them until they made a single, strong blade. Often they also fixed

▲ **Duels:** Viking warriors used their weapons against each other in duels. These formal fights with rules settled insults and arguments.

wedges of very hard – but brittle – iron along the sword's edges. Sharpening and polishing created a superb and beautiful weapon. Viking swords were very precious. His sword was usually the most valuable object a man owned, and could cost as much as 16 cows. Viking warriors gave their swords names such as 'Leg Biter' or 'Gold Hilt'.

The high cost of a sword meant that only the richest could afford them. Ordinary Vikings had to make do with humbler weapons such as spears. These were cheaper to make than

Within the forge the blacksmith beats
  The iron into a sword so long.
He carves a snake upon the blade
  And makes it bright and sharp and strong.
At last it's finished, and more polish
  Could not make it any brighter.
The chief is pleased: he swings it round
  And calls the sword 'the great Leg-Biter.'

swords because smiths needed only a little metal to forge the leaf-shaped points. Fixing them to long poles made powerful weapons.

Later Vikings also used axes, heavy weapons that took two hands to swing in battle. As well as spears or axes, Viking warriors carried long knives. These were used for fighting and for everyday tasks such as cutting up meat or sharpening wooden stakes.

Iron and other metals also went into armour. A Viking's light round wooden shield had a metal centre called a boss. This provided a sure grip and guarded the hand. Metal helmets and chain mail protected the wealthiest warriors. Both used a lot of metal, and mail was very slow to make. Armourers crafted it by linking thousands of tiny metal rings – as many as 40,000 for a full-length mail shirt.

Mail coat: hot and heavy to wear, but protected against swords and arrows

War axe: sometimes as richly decorated as a sword

Helmet: a costly piece of armour that poor warriors could not afford

Swords: so prized that poets wrote about them by name

Shield: could be up to 1 m (40 in) in diameter

Bravery and Berserkers

Viking stories are full of fighting because bravery in battle brought honour and fame. In fact, ordinary Viking men fought only if they went raiding, or if they got into a serious argument. There was a Scandinavian tradition that a fight to the death was the only way to settle the worst insults and disputes.

Only a few Vikings were full-time soldiers, protecting chieftains and kings, or serving in their armies. Of these warriors, the most terrifying were the beserkers. Hand-picked for their fighting skill and loyalty, they feared nothing. Working themselves up into a frightening rage, and possibly taking powerful drugs before a battle, they fought naked. A saga describing them says they 'bit their shields; they were as strong as bears or boars; they struck men down, but neither fire nor steel could mark them.' The fury of the berserkers was unforgettable: today, when someone seems to be filled with mad violence, we still say they have 'gone berserk'.

◄ **Warrior's gear:** armour and weapons were not just for protection and attack. Because of their expense, they showed off the owner's wealth and power.

12

Food and Farming

When Vikings celebrated, they slurped ale and greedily tucked in to steaming plates of beef.
Few meals were drunken feasts, however. In hungrier times, farming folk survived on bread
and salty cheese, or chewed on raw dried fish smeared with butter.

What Viking farmers ate depended on what they could grow, raise or catch. In the south, where crop plants grew well, everyone ate a lot of bread. It was coarse, solid stuff – heavier even than today's wholemeal bread. Women baked daily, for the bread quickly went stale. Farther north, meat was more important, and everywhere milk and cheese were an important part of meals.

Since metal was expensive, it was a lucky cook who owned an iron pot. Fortunately there were many other ways to heat food. Craftsmen carved pans from heatproof soapstone, or cut boiling pots from leather. The skin did not singe unless the water inside dried up.

Cooks also boiled food in pits lined with wood or hide. They filled the pits with water and threw in fire-heated stones.

▲ **Drinking:** cups made from cows' horns ended in a point, so drinkers could not put them down unless they had drained every last drop inside. Perhaps it's not surprising that so many sagas (Viking stories) describe wild parties! Fewer give details of how ill the drinkers must have felt the day after gulping down the rough home-brewed ale.

A water-filled pit four times the size of a bathtub boils in half an hour when heated this way. Hot rocks could cook in other ways, too. Packed around buried meat and covered with turf, they worked like a roasting oven.

Vikings were fond of barbecues! They grilled meat on a wood spit called a *steikja*. Today we still use this old Norse word in the English language when we talk about a wood 'stake' and a beef 'steak'.

Cooking wasn't always necessary – or even possible. When travelling or raiding, Vikings often survived on preserved food. They smeared butter on dried raw fish and chewed it. And they ate preserved raw meat, rather like modern Italian Parma ham or beef jerky.

Besides everyday drinks such as milk and water, Vikings had celebration drinks containing alcohol. Wine was scarce, imported and expensive, but ale made from barley was very popular. Heavy drinking was a regular part of special occasions, when the wealthiest drank from cows' horns.

As Eadred grows in hand and brain,
    He learns to use the sword to fight.
Even working in the fields
    He never lets it out of sight.
A wolf attacks, but Eadred's quick:
    He cuts one ear off – then the other.
His bravery makes him a hero:
    He saved the life of his small brother.

A Viking Farm

Storehouse: food was kept in semi-underground rooms, which were cooler in the summer months

Barn: used for storing crops

Privy: outside the main house, but not too far away

Forge: Viking farms were self-sufficient in everything, including a forge to make tools and weapons

Main house: the extended family, servants and slaves all lived under the same roof.

Stable: next to the house to help keep the animals warm in winter

Bathhouse: similar to a sauna today

Pigsty: Viking pigs lived on the left-over slops from the family food, much as pigs do today

Viking farms were working settlements, some very isolated. Besides the extended family, servants and slaves helped work the farm. Crops were grown in the surrounding fields and livestock such as chickens, geese and pigs were kept in the farmyard. Horses were mainly used for pulling carts and ploughs rather than ridden for transport.

Houses and Towns

Dark, smoky and busy, a Viking farmhouse was a family home packed into one room. When Viking settlers sailed west to seek a better life, they took with them their memories of home. In the new lands they found, they built the same long, ship-shaped houses.

Step inside a Viking house, and you'll find it very different from your own home. At first you'll struggle to see anything. The only light comes from the fire, and from the hole in the roof above that serves as a chimney. You can just make out two rows of stout wooden timbers that hold up the roof. As your eyes get used to the gloom, you realize that you are in a narrow room, about the length of a tennis court. People are all around you, for this is the *only* room in the house. Someone snores to your left on the raised earth floor that runs down both sides. A woman is cooking at the long peat fire right in front of you. Farther away, her daughter is weaving and her sister combs lice from a child's hair.

Step outside into the sunlight, and you can see that the house does not stand on its own. Nearby there's a storehouse for food, and a privy (lavatory). Not far away is

▲ **Houses:** near forests, and in the warmer parts of Scandinavia, most houses were made of wood. In colder northern regions, and where timber was scarce, the walls were earth or turf.

a barn for storing crops and a stable for sheltering animals in the winter. There is a bathhouse, like a modern sauna, and a forge. In the distance, close to the sea-shore, is the long, low outline of a boathouse. In most of Scandinavia, houses like these were far apart. This wasn't because Vikings didn't get on with their neighbours. It was because each farm needed a lot of grassland for feeding animals. Houses were closer together in the south, where crops grew well on the fertile land, so there were fewer grazing animals and farms could be smaller.

Only in Denmark were houses close enough to make what we'd call a village, but there were Viking towns scattered all over Scandinavia. They grew up in places where people gathered to trade. At town markets, local people sold what they had too much of and

His father's sick, and Eadred's soon
   The leader of the Viking band.
Their town is crowded, so he says:
   'We'll search for somewhere to expand.'
But which direction should they seek
   The land that is the very best?
To make the choice, he throws the sword:
   Its falling tip points to the west!

Chimney: a simple hole in the roof let smoke out and light in

Roof: made of wooden shingles

Doorway: the house had only one entrance and no windows

Walls: the frame and walls were made of stout wooden timbers

Fire: kept alight all the time, the peat fire was used for cooking and heat

Beds: there were no beds as we know them; instead, everyone slept on raised earth benches

▼ **Typical house:** Like most other Viking houses, this one has gently curving sides, much like an upturned ship. The shape is no coincidence. Early Viking houses probably had ships for roofs.

Animals: often lived in the house alongside people

Screens: light woven screens or hangings were sometimes used for privacy

bought what they lacked. The markets were also centres for selling slaves, and foreign goods such as wine, vegetable oil, honey, and glass. Foreign merchants who sold these took away in exchange valuable Viking products such as furs, feathers, walrus ivory (tusks) and amber – hardened tree resin that looked like clear yellow or orange plastic.

As the number of Viking people grew, trading towns got bigger. Farms, though, could not grow in the same way, because all the good land was already in use. Farmers settled on poorer land, higher on the mountain slopes, but there, farms had to be even bigger because there was less for animals to eat.

When even this land was farmed, the Vikings began to look for new lands to settle (see page 20). There were other reasons, though, why Viking settlers headed west across the Atlantic. Raiding had shown young men that they had the chance to make an exciting new life overseas. Better ships and sailing skills perhaps encouraged them, too. Or maybe they just wanted more freedom than they felt they had at home.

Ships and Shipbuilding

Viking shipbuilders started their work in the forest. They felled tall oaks and pines.
Then, using only simple hand tools, they chopped, shaved, nailed and knotted.
The trees became sleek, fast warships, or broad, strong cargo ships.

Viking shipwrights built many kinds of vessels, including broad trading ships and small flat-bottomed ferries. Their sleek longships are their most famous craft, however. These raiding ships were built long and narrow so they sailed fast. They had flat bottoms so their warrior crews could haul them up on a beach before a raid, and launch them quickly for a fast getaway. For speed at sea they had both a square sail and long oars.

When the crew rowed, the mast could be unstepped – taken down – so that it did not catch the breeze. This made the ship faster when rowing into the wind. A single ship could have as many as 50 oars. Viking warriors pulling on them sent the longship speeding through the water.

Inside the longships, planks ran the whole length to make a deck for the oarsmen. The planks were loose, so that it was easy to store supplies and equipment underneath. If the ship sprang a leak it took only an instant to remove the deck and bail (scoop out the sea water).

Longships were not just fast: they were beautiful too. The sails were dyed bright colours. The circular shields that hung above each oar were painted to match. Often there was an animal's head carved on the timber at the front. This ornament earned their ships the nickname 'dragon boats' among the terrified victims of Viking raids.

Trading ships or 'knarrs' were very different from longships. They needed much more storage space to carry bulky cargoes such as cattle or timber. Speed was not so important, so trading ships were shorter and broader than longships and sailed more slowly. They had decks only at the front and back. The crew loaded cargo into a hold (an area without deck planks) in the middle. Cargo ships were pure sailing ships: they had no oars and the mast was fixed.

Viking shipbuilders were experts at their trade. As well as building ships, they chose and cut timber in the forests. Each ship required about a dozen trees, with trunks a metre (40 in) across. For the keel (the ship's 'backbone'), they picked oaks with straight trunks 18 m (60 feet) high. For the other parts of

To find new lands they'll need strong ships
That can survive Atlantic gales.
The keels are laid, and Eadred watches
Shipwrights hammer home the nails.
Complete at last, the fine new ships
Fill the Viking folks with hope.
The sun glints on Leg-Biter's blade
As Eadred cuts the mooring rope.

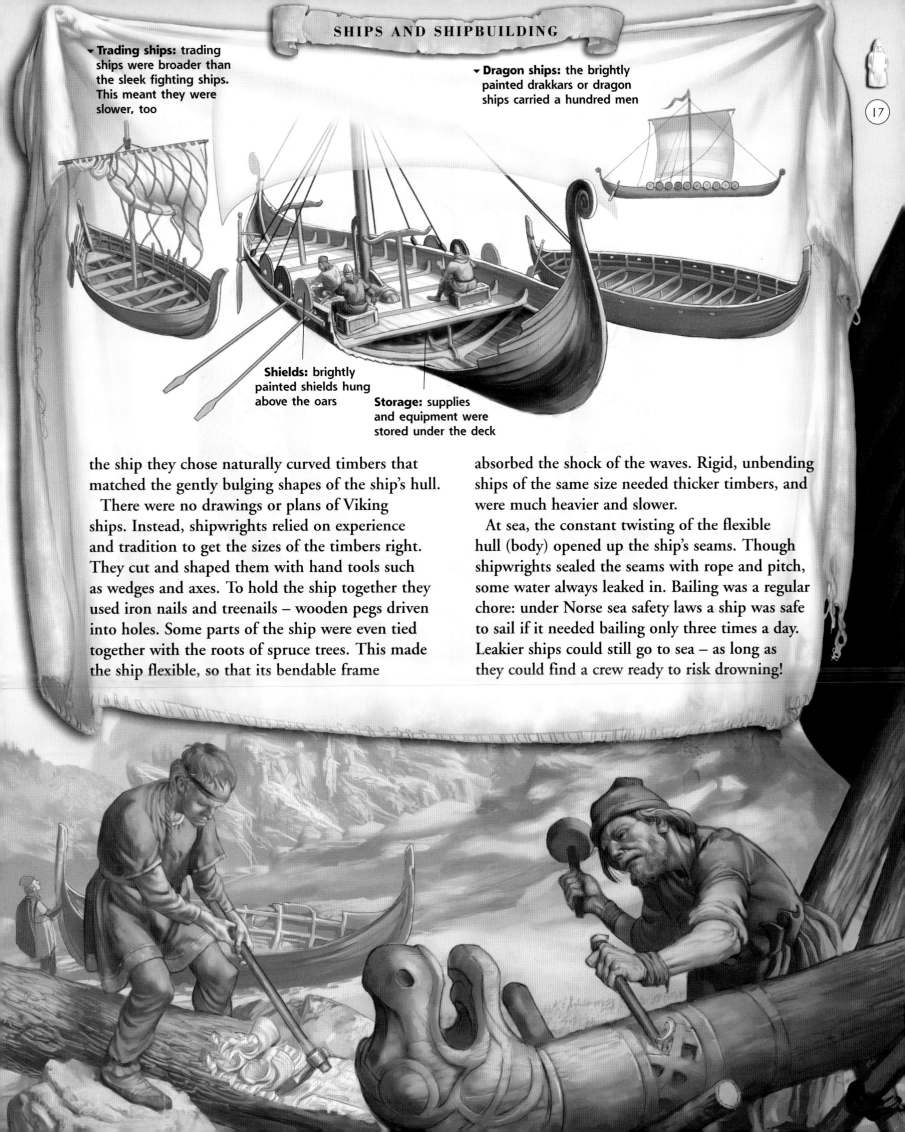

Trading ships: trading ships were broader than the sleek fighting ships. This meant they were slower, too

Dragon ships: the brightly painted drakkars or dragon ships carried a hundred men

Shields: brightly painted shields hung above the oars

Storage: supplies and equipment were stored under the deck

the ship they chose naturally curved timbers that matched the gently bulging shapes of the ship's hull.

There were no drawings or plans of Viking ships. Instead, shipwrights relied on experience and tradition to get the sizes of the timbers right. They cut and shaped them with hand tools such as wedges and axes. To hold the ship together they used iron nails and treenails – wooden pegs driven into holes. Some parts of the ship were even tied together with the roots of spruce trees. This made the ship flexible, so that its bendable frame

absorbed the shock of the waves. Rigid, unbending ships of the same size needed thicker timbers, and were much heavier and slower.

At sea, the constant twisting of the flexible hull (body) opened up the ship's seams. Though shipwrights sealed the seams with rope and pitch, some water always leaked in. Bailing was a regular chore: under Norse sea safety laws a ship was safe to sail if it needed bailing only three times a day. Leakier ships could still go to sea – as long as they could find a crew ready to risk drowning!

Sailing and Navigation

Guiding their ships on long ocean journeys, Viking mariners adjusted the sail and steered with a long oar. They found their way at sea by watching the sun, the stars, the wind and the waves – or by following birds and whales.

To make their ship speed through the salty ocean waves, Viking mariners spread a huge woollen sail against the wind. On a large ship the sail was 10 m (33 feet) square, and contained as much fabric as the clothes of the whole crew.

It was the sail that made a longship a deadly fighting machine. Until they began using sails around AD 650, Scandinavian people had to row everywhere. Even a short trip left the crew exhausted. Sails took much of the work out of ocean travel. They allowed Viking warriors to arrive at their destination fresh and ready to fight.

When raids were over, the sail made swift getaways possible. Viking ships were so fast and efficient that their victims could not chase them. As far as we know, no ships from France or England ever dared sail to raid the Viking coasts in revenge attacks.

Viking ships did not have rudders. To change direction, the longship

▸ **Styri:** Viking ships did not have rudders. To change direction, the longship crew instead pulled on a steering oar called a styri, which was fixed to the right-hand side of the ship.

crew instead pulled on a steering oar called a *styri*. (The side to which it was fixed was called *styrabord*, and in English, 'starboard' is still the name for the right-hand side of a ship.)

The sail helped in steering, too. By turning it carefully, the crew could sail in almost any direction. They could make rapid progress when the wind came from the side. They could even sail towards the wind. They did this by tacking – sailing in a zigzag pattern so that the wind always blew from one side or the other.

Guided by the stars and wind
They sail till land is out of sight.
Their journey's safe until a storm
Splits up the ships one dark, wet night.
Eadred's craft is nearly wrecked:
The crew is terrified they'll drown.
So with his trusty, shining sword
The captain hacks the tall mast down.

The first Viking mariners were afraid to sail out of sight of land. At dusk they sailed back to the shore and camped overnight. Once a ship had sailed the same course time and time again, the crew learned to identify landmarks on the coast, such as tall mountains. On their next trip they could use them to judge their progress and direction.

Sailing 'coastwise' like this is safe, but it stopped the Vikings crossing wide oceans. Because the Earth is curved, sailing away from the shore soon hides objects on land below the horizon – the line where sea meets sky. Just 7 km (4¹/2 miles) from the coast, low buildings on shore are hidden from view. Mountains take longer to vanish: a 300-m (1,000-ft) mountain is visible 60 km (40 miles) out to sea in clear weather. On a longer journey, all Viking mariners would see was the sea itself.

So how did they navigate (find their way)? We don't know for sure. However, we do know that they didn't use magnetic compasses (compasses with magnetized needles

▸ **Sun compass:** Viking crews could work out their latitude by using a simple sun compass like this one. To keep it level, the board was floated in a bowl of water. The noon sun shone on the central spike (called a gnomon) and cast a shadow. If the shadow was beyond the line drawn on the board, the ship was too far north; if the shadow was inside, the ship was too far south.

Steering by raven

Vikings also used ingenious tricks to find their way. When Floki Vilgerdarson sailed from The Faeroes to Iceland, he took on his ship three ravens (large black land birds). When he released the first, it flew back to the nearest land at Faeroe. Further on, he let the second go. It flew up, but returned to the ship and went to sleep on the sail because there was no land in sight. But the third bird flew higher and higher until it sighted land far ahead. Floki guessed it had seen Iceland, so he followed the bird and completed his journey safely.

that always point north). Archaeologists (people who dig up evidence of the past) have never found one with Viking remains. Nor did the Vikings use charts (sea maps). Instead they probably relied on the positions of the sun and the stars. These move in a regular, predictable way. Travelling north or south makes the stars' route across the sky slowly change.

Viking sailors probably also watched the winds and the ocean currents. These would have guided them even when clouds hid the sun and stars. And they would have known the routes that whales and seabirds followed, and used these to judge direction.

20

Exploration and Colonization

At the same time as Viking raiders began their bloody attacks, peaceful Norse people were starting to sail west. Braving the chilly Atlantic waves, they went in search of new, less crowded lands where they could farm and fish in freedom.

The Vikings' first stops were probably Orkney and Shetland. Half way between Norway and Scotland, these were the most northerly of the British Isles. They were convenient stopping-off points on the journey to Ireland, where Norse people settled from about AD 830.

The tiny Shetland and Orkney islands were hardly big enough for all the people who wanted to live there. So the Norse people launched their ships and headed farther west.

This time their target was The Faeroes, another group of small islands some 300 km (180 miles) away. Viking settlers who arrived there may have wondered whether it was worth making the journey. Whipped by angry Atlantic winds, The Faeroes were often also hidden in

◀ **Traders:** Viking traders also travelled east into Russia, and south to Constantinople in what is now Turkey.

thick fog, or soaked by torrential rain. Despite the savage climate, settlers made farms much like those of Norway. There were almost no trees, so they built homes of stone, turf, and driftwood. For heat and cooking they burned peat (dried bog moss).

The Faeroe settlers depended on friends, family and merchants in the Scandinavian homelands. Many things they needed were scarce or unobtainable on the islands. They looked forward eagerly to visits from supply ships for luxuries like glass and amber. Even vital materials such as wood and soapstone had to come in by ship.

It was not long before Viking explorers were again on their way west. Their next discovery must have been a pleasant surprise. Though the centre of the island they found was a barren place

> **Exploring west:**
> ── to the Orkney and Shetland Islands from *c.* AD 800
> ── to the Faeroe Islands from *c.* AD 860
> ── to Iceland *c.* AD 870
> ── Erik the Red's route to Greenland *c.* AD 985

Greenland

NORTH
ATLANTIC
OCEAN

Iceland

The Faeroes

Orkney   Shetland

Ireland   British   Scandinavia
          Isles

of ice and volcanoes, there was woodland and plenty of grassland on the coast.

Compared to The Faeroes, it looked good. Perhaps too good. One of the first settlers, Floki Vilgerdarson (see page 19), unwisely spent his first enjoyable summer hunting, instead of cutting hay. When winter set in, his animals starved and he barely survived. In memory of that first, harsh winter he named his new home 'Iceland'.

Many more settlers followed Floki, and within just a few years there were farms on all the good land. The new settlers burned down many of the forests to create more pasture. They thrived, and ate well. However, we would call them poor – they had few possessions.

The tale of the Norsemen's last great island discovery begins around 985. That year a Norwegian murderer, Erik the Red, came to Iceland. His temper was as fiery red as his beard and hair, and it wasn't long before he killed again. Looking for somewhere new to run to, Erik heard an old story. Sixty years earlier, gales had blown a ship off course. The captain saw an island land far to the west, but did not land there. Erik chose this land as his new home, and crossed the icy ocean to its

shores. After exploring, he returned to Iceland to get others to follow him. To encourage them, he named the place 'the Green Land', thinking it would sound more inviting than Iceland.

The trick worked, and 25 ships set sail. However, the settlers who completed the voyage discovered that Erik's land was anything but green. It was treeless and barren. Only the southern and western shores were worth settling. Even there, life was harsh. Starving settlers sucked every trace of meat from the bones they gnawed on. Still hungry, they cracked the bones to get at the marrow inside.

No wonder, then, that when news came of another new land, again to the west, there were Greenlanders who were eager to explore it.

Without a sail the voyagers
    Are at the mercy of the sea.
Thirst and hunger wear them down
    As they drift on so aimlessly.
But then, at last, a bird they spy,
    And weeds, and wood, and at last land!
To claim the island, Eadred thrusts
    His sword into the golden sand.

Clothing and Jewellery

Vikings loved beautiful things. They decorated their clothes with bright colours and patterned borders. They fastened them using huge brooches carved with fantastic beasts and knotted lines. Market towns became craft centres for the jewellers who made these ornaments of gold and silver.

One craft, however, took place in every home. All Viking women spun, wove, dyed and sewed to make clothes. They also made huge pieces of cloth, for sails, tents and wagon covers. Their raw materials were the stems of hemp or flax plants or, more often, wool clipped and plucked from a sheep's back.

Turning these fibres into cloth was slow work. Making a woollen sail for a ship took as much time and as many people as building the ship from wood.

Making enough fabric for a shirt or a cloak was quicker, of course. Even these clothes took time, however, especially if the cloth was decorated. Colour was the commonest way to do this. Women dyed the threads or the fabric using plants. Lady's bedstraw and madder gave wool a red colour. Woad made a blue dye, and walnut made brown. Lichens gave shades of purple and yellow. Woven from different coloured threads, Viking clothes could be very bright.

▲ **Wool and wood:** two of the main raw materials Vikings used to create colourful clothes and ornate carved wooden objects.

There were other ways to make clothes more attractive. Weavers knotted long loose threads into the cloth to make it shaggy and warm. Or they made braid in raised patterns, sometimes using gold or silver threads, to decorate the edges. From lengths of the cloth, Viking women cut out the shapes they needed for garments. The simplest, such as cloaks, needed little shaping and sewing, but others were more carefully fitted.

For themselves, they sewed linen chemises (long shirts), which they wore next to the skin, and long wool dresses to wear on top. In cold weather women added a shawl or cloak, or an apron when working. Men wore wool trousers and tunics, with linen pants and shirt underneath. Thick capes or animal skins and furs kept everyone warm.

To fasten these clothes, both men and women used big brooches. Here, too, they showed their love of pattern and decoration. Patterns swirl

The years on Greenland swiftly pass.
　　The Vikings thrive and build their town.
But Eadred's old and cold and tired –
　　His death seems near as he lies down.
His wife swears that she'll bury him
　　With clothes and treasure – and his swords.
'Not my beloved Leg-Biter!
　　It's Guthrum's now!' are his last words.

and weave around Viking brooches, and fantastic snarling beasts poke their heads from every corner.

Simple brooches were made of bronze, but wealthier Vikings wore brooches and other jewellery of gold and silver. They were often decorated with precious stones, crystals, amber, or glass. Women wore arm and finger rings and thick neck rings of gold or silver. These were not just for show. They were also a convenient way to carry money. Vikings did not use coins or banks. A silver neck ring was the Norse equivalent of wallet bulging with banknotes.

These precious and beautiful objects were made by skilled smiths (metalworkers). Every Viking farm had an iron smithy for making and repairing tools and weapons, but the craft of jewellery-making was rarer. Jewellers

▲ **Spinning and woodcarving:** women spun wool thread using a drop spindle (one was found at L'Anse aux Meadows – see page 31), which they then wove into cloth. Men made many beautiful and ornate carved wooden objects.

gathered in the market towns that grew up around the Scandinavian coasts. Rich customers gave them gold, silver and jewels to make into fine pieces of art. Though they were made a thousand years ago, these treasures still look amazing.

Despite their skills, Viking jewellers earned little respect. They were nicknamed 'cinder blowers' and despised for their faces blackened by their fires. In a world where warfare and success in battle meant everything, the most magnificent gold jewellery was worth less than a fine iron sword.

Magic and Religion

In Viking myth, the world was flat, like a plate. The gods at its centre battled with evil giants who lived around the edge. Humans were trapped between them. Beneath the ground dwelled dwarfs and fantastic serpents roamed the seas.

Norse people worshipped in the grand halls of their lords and kings, by swampy lakes, near rocky crags, and among sacred trees. When they needed help, they made sacrifices to the gods, killing animals or even people in their honour. Sacrifices to Thor kept away famine or disease. Odin protected them from war, and Frey's blessing was essential at weddings. Feasting followed all these ceremonies.

Religion was a private thing, too. Many people wore lucky amulets to keep the gods with them at all times. These amulets were small bronze, ivory or silver images of gods or their signs. The most popular of all was Thor's hammer.

Vikings held solemn ceremonies when someone died. They buried the dead with their possessions, sometimes marking the grave with a mound of earth or a ship-shaped ring of stones. Wealthy people and leaders got special burials.

▲ **Amulet:** though the Viking people became Christians, many of them clung to their old ways. They went to church and prayed at the cross, but at home they were still pagan. A few wore amulets lilke this one that combined the cross with Thor's hammer. After all, for a people who believed in many gods, there was always room for one more.

Their horses and dogs were killed and buried with them, often inside a real ship. Sometimes their slaves or wives were sacrificed too.

Not all Vikings were buried. Some were cremated (burned). Their relatives bent their weapons and armour in the hot ash. Cremation in a ship showed special respect: lit and launched, it carried the dead man to the spirit world in a crackling blaze.

These ceremonies ended when the Christian religion spread among Viking people. Settlers in Christian countries such as England and France were the first to give up their pagan (non-Christian) ways. Then King Harald Bluetooth (*c.* 910–85) became a Christian and encouraged his Danish people to follow him. In Norway, King (later Saint) Olaf (995–1030) preferred force to persuasion. He cruelly killed those who would not become Christians. Iceland adopted Christianity as its official religion around AD 1000, and Erik the Red's son, Leif, took the religion to Greenland.

The people mourn their leader's death
  In a church right by the shore.
With Christian chants they bless his soul –
  But bury him with prayers to Thor!
Then Guthrum grabs the famous sword
  And speaks of his long-held ambition.
'Father, I won't let you down –
  I'll lead another expedition!'

The Viking Gods

Though Norse people worshipped many gods, they had special respect for three of them.

Thor: the greatest of all the Viking gods, Thor was a storm god who lived in the sky. He made the wind, the rain and the sunshine. His sign was a hammer, which stood for the thunderbolts that he hurled at those who displeased him. Immensely strong, he fought with giants. Thursday is named after him.

Odin: war god, poet and sorcerer, Odin could disguise himself by changing his shape. He rode an eight-legged horse called Sleipnr, and had a spear that never missed its target. Two ravens that sat on his shoulders told him everything he needed to know. Called Woden in England, he gave his name to Wednesday.

Frey: the fertility god Frey blessed love and marriage. With his help, the crops grew and the meadows provided masses of hay. Frey had a magic ship called Skidbladnir, and a boar named Goldbristlesii. According to legend, Frey married the giantess Gerd, and their children began one of the families that ruled in Sweden. Many places in Sweden are still named after the god.

To America!

Sailing for Greenland, a Viking knarr gets lost in fog. When the weather clears, a new land looms to the west. It's too flat and wooded to be Greenland, so captain Bjarni Herjolfsson sails away . . . and misses the chance to be the first European in America!

Bjarni lost his way in about AD 985, and for fifteen years Greenlanders talked about the new land he had seen from afar. Then one of them decided to do more than talk. His name was Leif Eriksson. His father, Erik the Red, had discovered Greenland by following the route of a ship that was blown off course. Now Leif saw that he had the chance of discovering another new land in much the same way.

He gathered a crew of 35 and bought Bjarni's ship from him. Then he set off from the chilly Greenland shore. We don't know Leif's route, or where he landed, but we can guess. At first he probably sailed not west but north, up the Davis Strait. This stretch of ocean separates Greenland from North America. Then, turning west, he sighted land and went ashore. Finding a coast of bare rock, with glaciers (huge rivers of ice) behind, he called the land Helluland (Norse for 'Stone-Slab Land').

Sailing on, Leif and his men found another coastline. This time it had white sand beaches and forests, so Leif named it Forest Land (Markland in Norse). It was probably the coast of modern Labrador.

Still not satisfied, Leif and his men continued south. When they reached what we now call Newfoundland, they found a place that seemed ideal for settlement. They went ashore and drank the dew from the grass 'and thought they had never tasted anything as sweet'. Big salmon leaped in the rivers; the climate was mild, and so much grass grew in winter that haymaking wasn't necessary.

Leif's adventurers set up camp on the shore, and spent the winter there. As they explored the land around their camp, one of them, Tyrker, made an amazing discovery. He found berries that were very much like the grapes that grew near his ancestors' home in Germany. Delighted, Leif named the new land Vinland ('Wine Land').

When spring came, Leif and his crew packed up their belongings. They loaded their ship with timber and 'grapes', and sailed back to Greenland, where their discoveries caused great excitement.

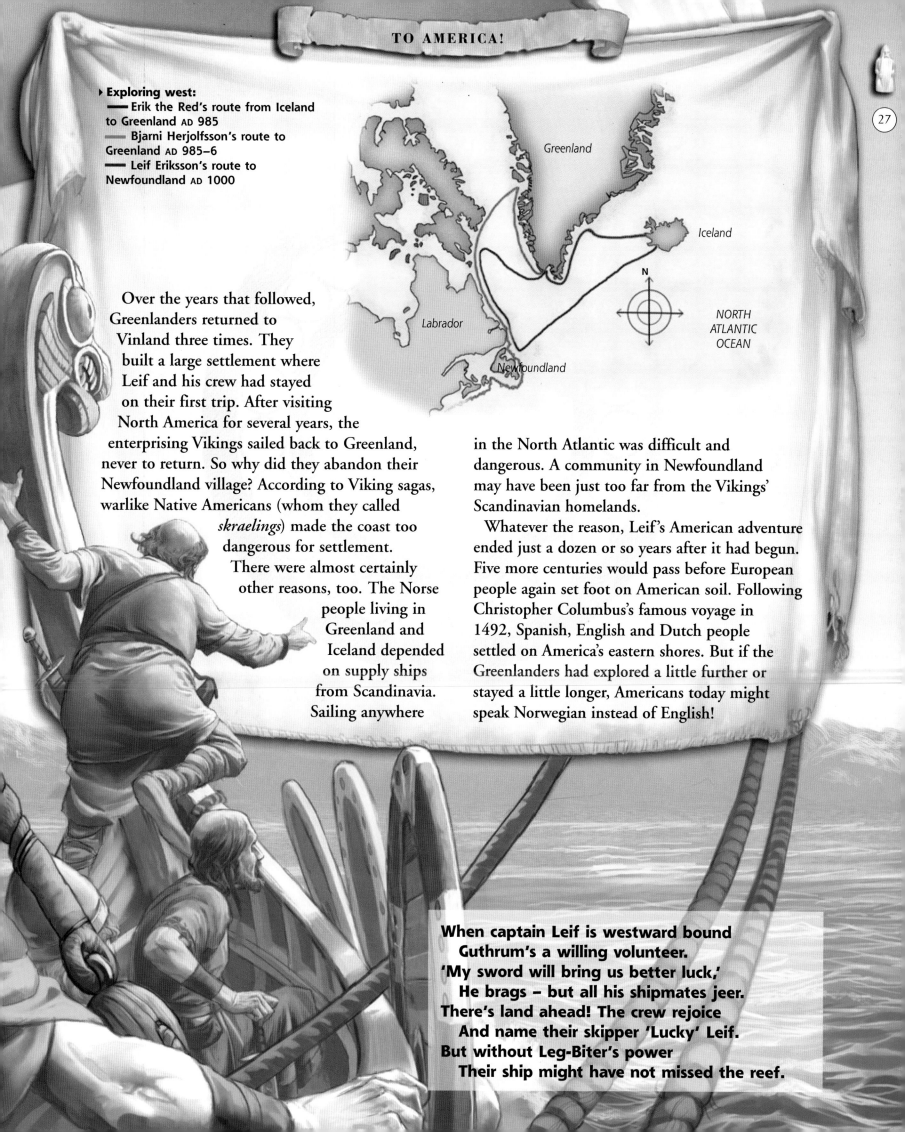

Exploring west:
—— Erik the Red's route from Iceland to Greenland AD 985
—— Bjarni Herjolfsson's route to Greenland AD 985–6
—— Leif Eriksson's route to Newfoundland AD 1000

Greenland

Iceland

Labrador

N

NORTH ATLANTIC OCEAN

Newfoundland

Over the years that followed, Greenlanders returned to Vinland three times. They built a large settlement where Leif and his crew had stayed on their first trip. After visiting North America for several years, the enterprising Vikings sailed back to Greenland, never to return. So why did they abandon their Newfoundland village? According to Viking sagas, warlike Native Americans (whom they called *skraelings*) made the coast too dangerous for settlement. There were almost certainly other reasons, too. The Norse people living in Greenland and Iceland depended on supply ships from Scandinavia. Sailing anywhere in the North Atlantic was difficult and dangerous. A community in Newfoundland may have been just too far from the Vikings' Scandinavian homelands.

Whatever the reason, Leif's American adventure ended just a dozen or so years after it had begun. Five more centuries would pass before European people again set foot on American soil. Following Christopher Columbus's famous voyage in 1492, Spanish, English and Dutch people settled on America's eastern shores. But if the Greenlanders had explored a little further or stayed a little longer, Americans today might speak Norwegian instead of English!

When captain Leif is westward bound
    Guthrum's a willing volunteer.
'My sword will bring us better luck,'
    He brags – but all his shipmates jeer.
There's land ahead! The crew rejoice
    And name their skipper 'Lucky' Leif.
But without Leg-Biter's power
    Their ship might have not missed the reef.

28

Runes, Myths and Legends

When Norse people wanted their words to live longer than an echo, they wrote them down in runes.
Carved in spiky letters on wood or stone, some of these short messages have lasted a thousand years.
Vikings kept longer stories and legends alive by repeating them to their children as sagas.

Carving words might seem to be a difficult way to write, but for the Vikings it was no harder than using a pen and ink. A thousand years ago, European writers had neither paper nor ready-made ink and pens. Before scribes (professional writers) could start work, they had to scrape smooth and rule parchment made of sheepskin. Then they mixed ink from water, soot and gum. They even had to cut their pens from goose feathers. By contrast, rune-carvers needed only a strip of wood and a knife to get going.

The shapes of rune letters made them easy to carve in wood. Wood has a grain – tough and softer layers that show which way the tree grew. If the lines of runes went the same way as the grain they would be hard to see. To avoid this, the letters used only vertical (upright) and slanting lines. There are no curves, because these were not easy to cut with a simple tool.

Rune writing used an alphabet of just 16 letters. There were no letters for D, G or P, even though Scandinavians used these sounds when they spoke. There were two ways to write the sound we call A, but no letters for E or O.

Despite these drawbacks, the Norse people used runes widely. They changed the rune alphabet to make it better for writing on stone, bone and metal. These materials rot slowly, so carvings on them have lasted to the present day – long after most wood runes have decayed.

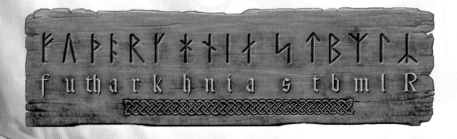

◄ **Rune alphabet:** Together, the 16 letters were called the futhark, after the sounds of the first six. This Norse name is just like the English word 'alphabet', which comes from the Greek name for its first two letters: alpha (A) and beta (B).

As they load their ship with timber,
  Guthrum's nowhere near the dunes.
He's busy scratching on a stone
  A message written all in runes.
He jumps on board and they set sail
  Through the spray and freezing rain.
They wonder as they pull the oars
  If they will see their homes again.

Rune Writings

Rune signs marked boundaries, roads and bridges. When Vikings who could write made or owned something, they marked it with a rune. And they sometimes recorded magic formulas (recipes) in runes. Most often, though, runes were used on stones as memorials, like this one from Sjörup, in northern Denmark:

Saxi put up this stone in memory of his
comrade Asbjorn, Toki's son.
He did not flee at [the battle of] Uppsala,
But fought while he could hold weapons.

▸ **Sagas:** Vikings enjoyed listening to a good saga, especially on long, dark winter evenings.

A few rune stones record fairly long poems, but most of Viking literature was not written down (at least, not at first). Instead, the Norse people simply remembered it, passing on their history, poems, stories, and legends in speech.

Two or three centuries after the Viking age, writers began to copy down all this spoken wisdom and art. They recorded the Viking myths and traditions as sagas. Some of the sagas read like fairy stories. Filled with gods, kings and monsters, they are glorious stories of Viking victories. Some sagas, though, are much more like history. They are written records of past events.

Though sagas tell us a lot about the Viking age, it's a mistake to rely on them too much. Some sagas record the bragging voices of proud men. Others give a one-sided view. Nevertheless, sagas are an important source of knowledge about the Viking era. For some events, such as the voyages to America, they were for a long time the only proof of the real-life deeds of daring Viking heroes.

The Sword Unearthed

How do we know what the Viking world was like? Runes and sagas give us an entertaining picture of how the Vikings saw themselves. But it's through archaeology that we can piece together the past and really see how they lived.

The Vikings ended their terrifying raids nearly 1,000 years ago. Their grandchildren mostly became peace-loving farmers and sailors in the lands their ancestors had settled or conquered. Before long the famous war swords were lost; Viking graves and houses collapsed and disappeared under ploughed fields.

The Vikings themselves were gone, but they were not forgotten. Nor were traces of their lives completely wiped out by the passing centuries. The Vikings were remembered in writings of their time, such as the stories of the Viking raids recorded by their victims (see pages 6–7). Rune stones and sagas also tell us much about the Vikings and their world.

The remains of Viking homes, graves and possessions have stories to tell, too. Understanding them is the job of archaeologists – scientists who study of what's left of people of the past. Archaeology has provided the details that really bring the Viking age to life.

Viking burials have been a great source of knowledge. While they were still pagans, Vikings buried their dead with their possessions, sometimes in boats. So when archaeologists discover burial sites, they can learn a lot about the personal world of Vikings, and perhaps about how they sailed, too.

Some ship discoveries have been remarkably well preserved. The Oseberg ship, for example, named after the Norwegian farm on which it was found in 1904, is an almost perfectly preserved Viking chief's coastal ship. Inside were the remains of beds, sleighs, looms, tents, a cooking pot, a bail bucket, and a beautifully carved cart. Near the remains of the princess who was buried in the ship was the skeleton of another young woman, possibly a servant, and of ten horses and cattle sacrificed at the funeral. The ship has been carefully reconstructed, and you can still see it and the treasures it contained, at the Viking Ships Museum just outside the Norwegian capital, Oslo.

The remains of Viking ships have helped archaeologists in another way. By carefully studying the planks and beams, it is possible to build exact replicas of the vessels. Mariners have sailed

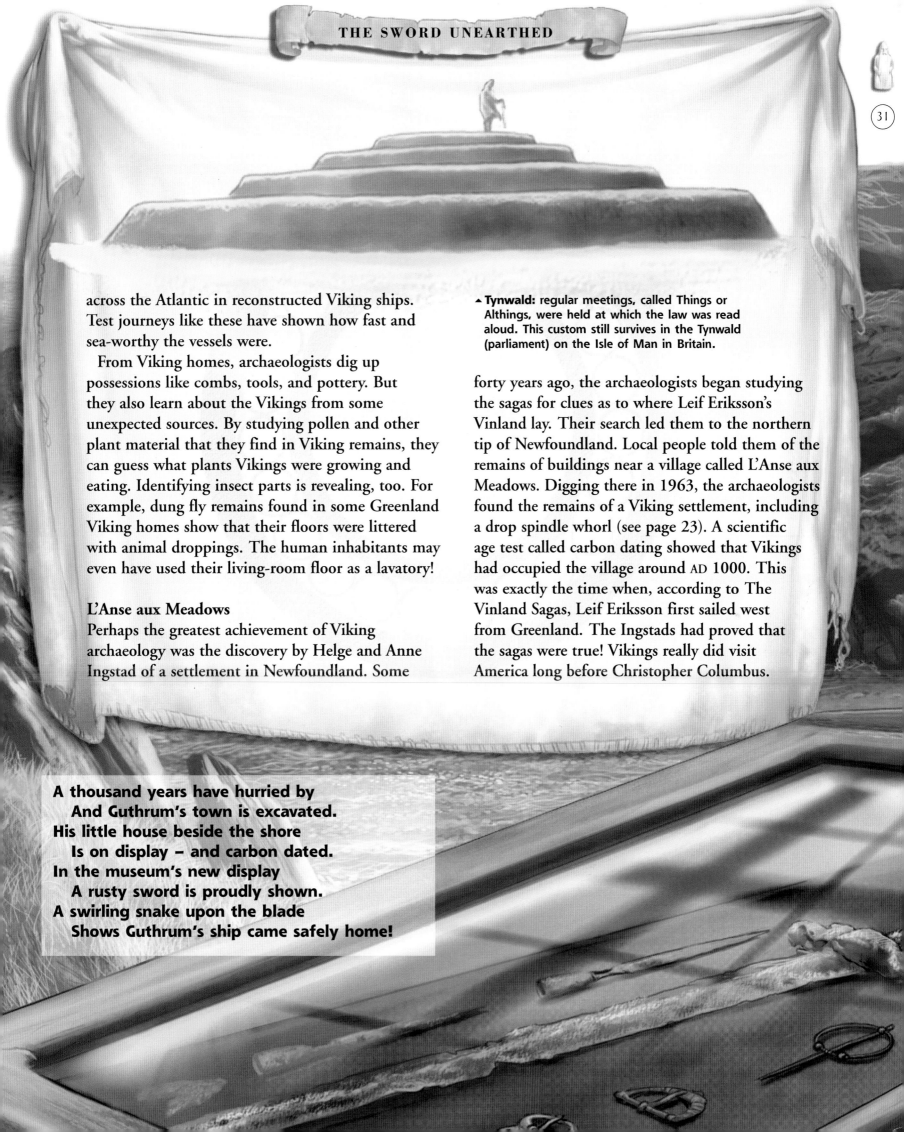

across the Atlantic in reconstructed Viking ships. Test journeys like these have shown how fast and sea-worthy the vessels were.

From Viking homes, archaeologists dig up possessions like combs, tools, and pottery. But they also learn about the Vikings from some unexpected sources. By studying pollen and other plant material that they find in Viking remains, they can guess what plants Vikings were growing and eating. Identifying insect parts is revealing, too. For example, dung fly remains found in some Greenland Viking homes show that their floors were littered with animal droppings. The human inhabitants may even have used their living-room floor as a lavatory!

L'Anse aux Meadows

Perhaps the greatest achievement of Viking archaeology was the discovery by Helge and Anne Ingstad of a settlement in Newfoundland. Some

▲ **Tynwald:** regular meetings, called Things or Althings, were held at which the law was read aloud. This custom still survives in the Tynwald (parliament) on the Isle of Man in Britain.

forty years ago, the archaeologists began studying the sagas for clues as to where Leif Eriksson's Vinland lay. Their search led them to the northern tip of Newfoundland. Local people told them of the remains of buildings near a village called L'Anse aux Meadows. Digging there in 1963, the archaeologists found the remains of a Viking settlement, including a drop spindle whorl (see page 23). A scientific age test called carbon dating showed that Vikings had occupied the village around AD 1000. This was exactly the time when, according to The Vinland Sagas, Leif Eriksson first sailed west from Greenland. The Ingstads had proved that the sagas were true! Vikings really did visit America long before Christopher Columbus.

A thousand years have hurried by
  And Guthrum's town is excavated.
His little house beside the shore
  Is on display – and carbon dated.
In the museum's new display
  A rusty sword is proudly shown.
A swirling snake upon the blade
  Shows Guthrum's ship came safely home!

Index